UR

David Carr Glover
METHOD for PIANO

THEORY

Martha Mier and
June Montgomery
with David Carr Glover

The knowledge of note reading, intervals, rhythm, music symbols and terms, and the ability to listen are essential to the development of a strong foundation for the piano student.

This THEORY book was written to help provide this foundation by giving students reinforcement of the concepts presented in the LESSONS book of the David Carr Glover METHOD for PIANO. As the students advance in their ability to play the piano, the THEORY book will help give them a better understanding of the music they are performing.

The pages are designed to be interesting and fun for the students in order to spark their enthusiasm and increase their motivation.

Teachers, please notice that the answers and musical examples for use with the listening exercises are found in the back of this book.

THEORY, Level Four, is directly correlated with LESSONS, Level Four, of the David Carr Glover METHOD for PIANO.

Design and Illustrations: Jeannette Aquino
Editor: Carole Flatau
Production Coordinator: Sonja Poorman

Contents

Supplementary materials correlated with
LESSONS, Level Four, from the
David Carr Glover METHOD for PIANO

Music Symbols and Terms
(Review)

1. On the line after each definition below, write the number of the matching symbol or term shown on the rocket.

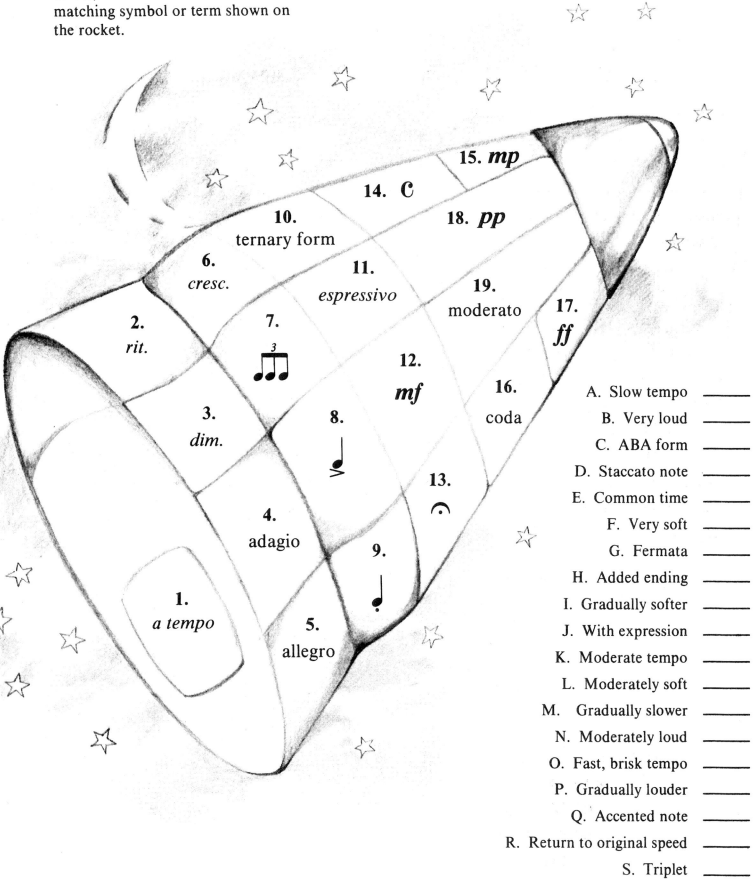

A. Slow tempo _____
B. Very loud _____
C. ABA form _____
D. Staccato note _____
E. Common time _____
F. Very soft _____
G. Fermata _____
H. Added ending _____
I. Gradually softer _____
J. With expression _____
K. Moderate tempo _____
L. Moderately soft _____
M. Gradually slower _____
N. Moderately loud _____
O. Fast, brisk tempo _____
P. Gradually louder _____
Q. Accented note _____
R. Return to original speed _____
S. Triplet _____

2. Name this scale. Play.

_____ _____ _____ Scale

3. Write the Roman numeral names of the chords in this A minor chord progression. Play.

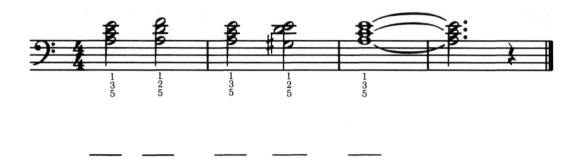

____ ____ ____ ____ ____

4. Tap and count:

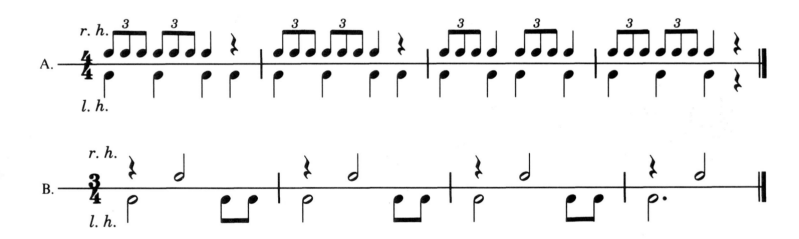

5. On the line below each triad, write **root** for root position triad, **1st** for first inversion triad, or **2nd** for second inversion triad.

____ ____ ____ ____ ____ ____ ____

Use with pages 4-5, LESSONS, Level Four.

6. Write the beats under these measures. Clap and count aloud.

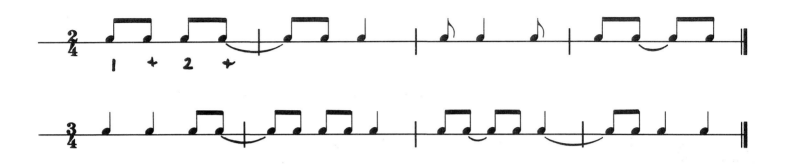

7. Play the melody below. Using the C major chord progression, play chords with the left hand as indicated.

FRANKIE AND JOHNNY

AMERICAN FOLK SONG

Use with pages 6-7, LESSONS, Level Four.

Sixteenth Notes and Rests

A single sixteenth note has two flags. ♪ A sixteenth rest has two flags. ♪

Two or more sixteenth notes may be connected by a double beam.

When the quarter note receives one beat, the sixteenth note receives one-fourth beat.

In ²⁄₄ , ³⁄₄ or ⁴⁄₄ time, four 16th notes = 1 quarter note, two 16th notes = one 8th note.

Note	Rest	Value
♪	♪	one-fourth beat
♫	♪	one-half beat
♬	♪	one beat

8. Write four groups of sixteenth notes as shown in the example.

9. Write four sixteenth rests.

How to Count Sixteenth Notes
(Your teacher will tell you how to count.)

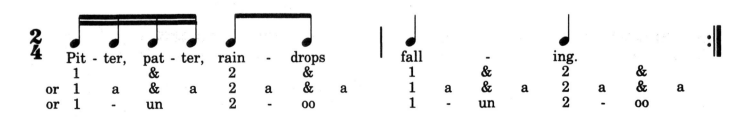

	Pit - ter,	pat - ter,	rain -	drops		fall	-	ing.		
	1	&	2	&		1	&	2	&	
or 1	a	& a	2	a &	a	1	a &	a 2	a &	a
or 1	-	un	2	- oo		1	-	un	2	- oo

Use with page 8, LESSONS, Level Four.

10. Write the counts under these notes.

__   _   _   _   _   __   _   _   _

11. Tap and count:

12. In each line, A and B, there is one box of notes or rests that does not match the other four in that line. Cross out the box that doesn't match.

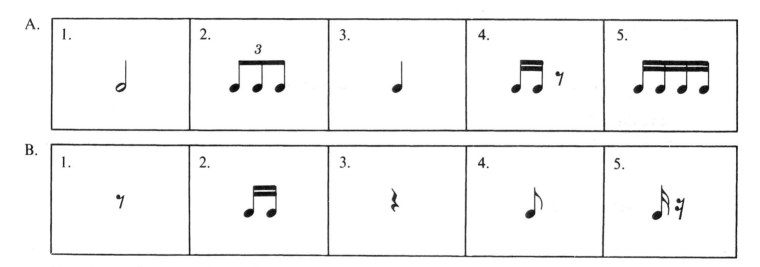

13. * Look and listen as your teacher plays one of the rhythm patterns in each line, A and B. Which rhythm pattern do you hear? Circle 1 or 2.

A. 1.   2.

B. 1.   2.

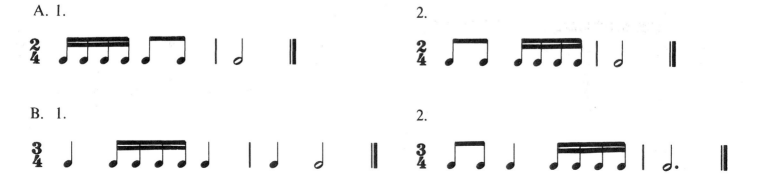

Use with page 8, LESSONS, Level Four.

Key of D Minor (Review)

14. Write the chord letter names above the staff for this chord progression in the key of D minor. Write the Roman numerals below the staff. Play this chord progression.

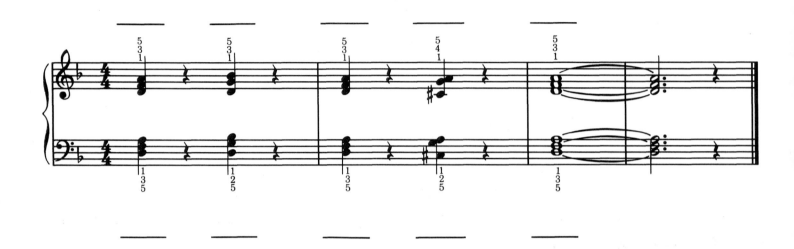

15. Add the necessary accidentals (♯ , ♭ or ♮) to change these D natural minor scales as indicated. Play each scale.

D HARMONIC MINOR SCALE: (Raise the 7th tone ½ step.)

D MELODIC MINOR SCALE: (Raise the 6th and 7th tones ½ step **ascending,** then lower them **descending.**)

16. Fill in the blanks.

    A. The key signature for the key of D minor is _____ _____.

    B. The relative major key for D minor is _____ major.

17. Using the rhythm below, play the primary chords in the key of D minor as indicated by the Roman numerals.

Use with page 9, LESSONS, Level Four.

Key of A Major

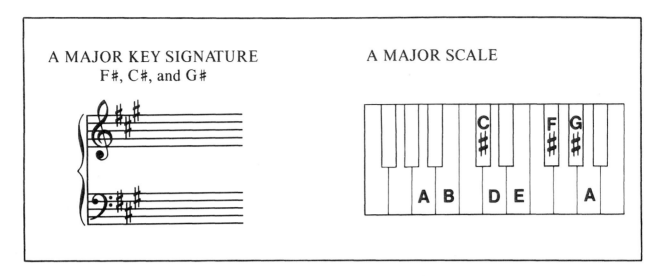

A MAJOR KEY SIGNATURE
F#, C#, and G#

A MAJOR SCALE

18. Write the A Major key signature on each grand staff below.

19. Use quarter notes to write the ascending A Major scale. Play the scale with right hand and left hand ascending and descending.

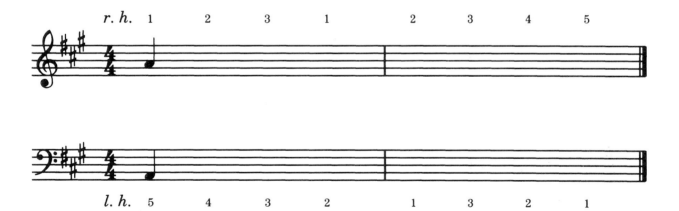

20. Fill in the blanks.

A. The key signature for A Major has _____ sharps.

B. The notes that are sharped are named _____ , _____ , and _____ .

Use with page 10, LESSONS, Level Four.

Primary Chords in A Major

21. Play these A Major primary chords.

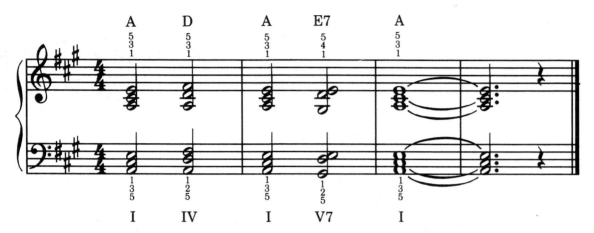

22. Copy the primary chords in A Major from above. Write the chord letter name on the blank above each chord, and the Roman numeral on the blank below each chord.

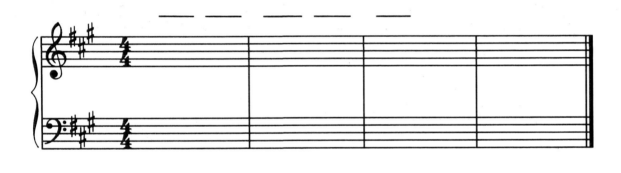

23. Write the notes of the **first inversion** and **second inversion chords** for the root position A Major triad. Play the root position and both inversions with each hand.

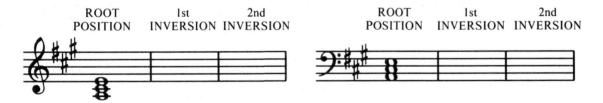

24. Write the correct Roman numeral under each primary chord in A Major.

Use with page 10, LESSONS, Level Four.

25. Play these blocked and broken chords.

ALBERTI BASS is an accompaniment form that consists of broken chords played in the style written below.

26. Play this Alberti bass accompaniment. Transpose to the keys of G, D, and A Major.

27. Write the Alberti bass in the bass clef. Play and transpose to the key of A Major.

Adapted from "Etude," LESSONS, Level Four, page 11

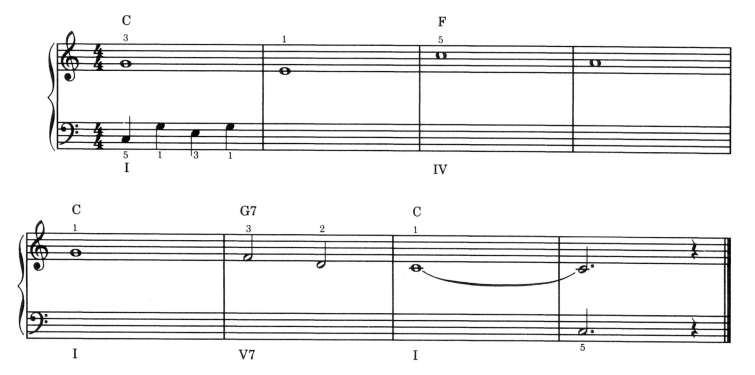

Use with page 11, LESSONS, Level Four.

First Inversion Triads (Review)

28. Name the root of each **first inversion triad.** If the triad is minor, add a small **m** following the chord letter name.

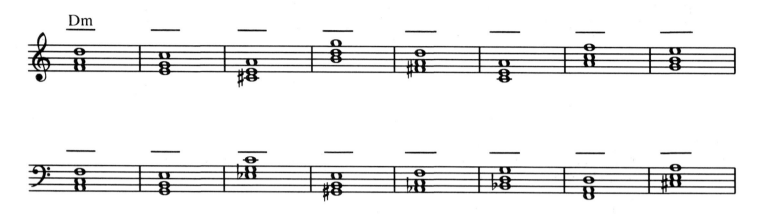

29. Write the **first inversion triad** in the blank measure following each root position triad.

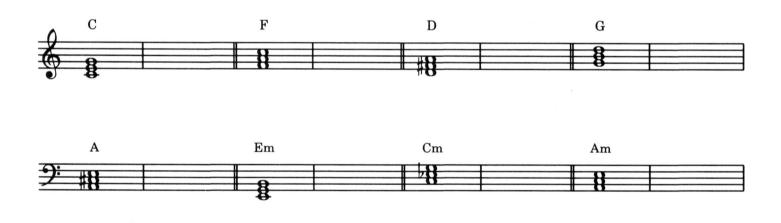

30. Write the name of the root above each triad. Circle each **first inversion triad.**

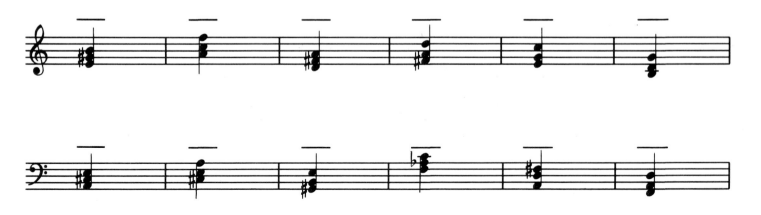

Use with pages 13-15, LESSONS, Level Four.

31. Find the minor scale related to G Major. Circle the 6th tone of the G Major scale.

32. The name of that note is _____ .

33. Write the notes of the ascending **natural minor scale** related to G Major, using the same key signature as G Major (one sharp, F#). Use quarter notes. Play this scale.

34. On the keyboard write the letter names of the **natural minor scale** related to G Major.

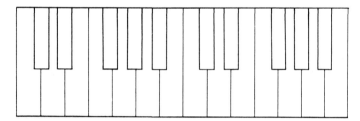

E Harmonic Minor Scale

35. Using quarter notes, write the notes of the ascending **E harmonic minor scale.** (Raise the 7th tone of the E natural minor scale.) Play this scale.

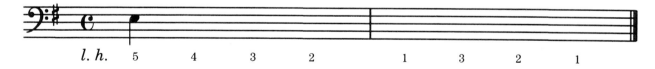

36. On the keyboard write the letters of the E **harmonic minor scale.**

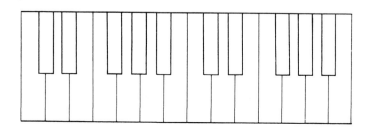

Use with pages 16-17, LESSONS, Level Four.

37. Use quarter notes to write the E MELODIC MINOR SCALE. (Raise the 6th and 7th tones of the E natural minor scale going up and lower the 6th and 7th tones coming down.) Play this scale.

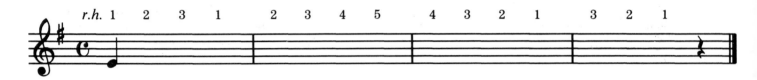

38. On the keyboard write the letters of the E melodic minor scale going up.

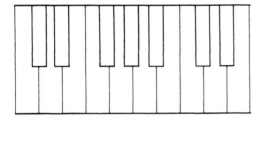

39. On the keyboard write the letters of the E melodic minor scale coming down.

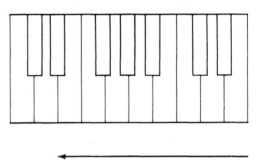

40. * Look and listen as your teacher plays these three minor scales. On the line in front of each scale write the order in which your teacher plays them. For example, write number **1** in front of the scale played first.

A.   E HARMONIC MINOR SCALE

B.   E MELODIC MINOR SCALE

C.   E NATURAL MINOR SCALE

Use with pages 16-17, LESSONS, Level Four.

Primary Chords in E Minor

The primary chords in the KEY OF E MINOR are formed by using the notes of the E HARMONIC MINOR SCALE.

41. Build triads on the 1st, 4th and 5th tones of the E harmonic minor scale.

42. Play this E minor chord progression.

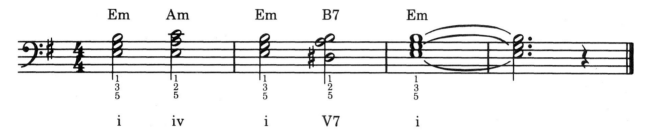

43. Write the Roman numeral name of these primary chords in the key of E minor.

___ ___ ___ ___   ___ ___ ___ ___

44. Write the primary chords as indicated in the bass clef, then play this piece.

Adapted from "A RUSSIAN STORY," LESSONS, Level Four, page 19.

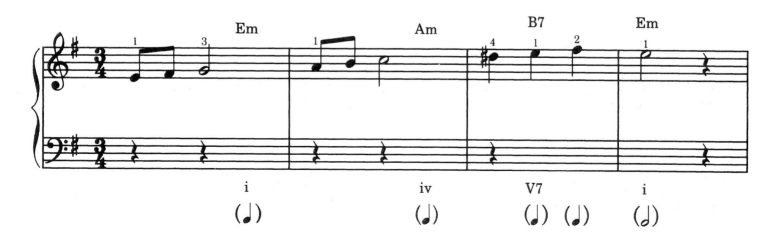

Use with pages 18-19, LESSONS, Level Four.

45. Name the root of each **second inversion triad.** If the chord is minor, write a small **m** following the chord letter name.

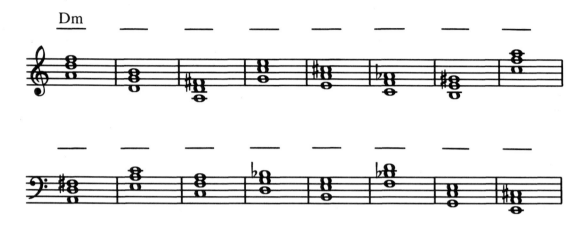

46. On the blank above each keyboard, write the letter name of the root of the chord. Circle the keyboard if the chord is in **second inversion.**

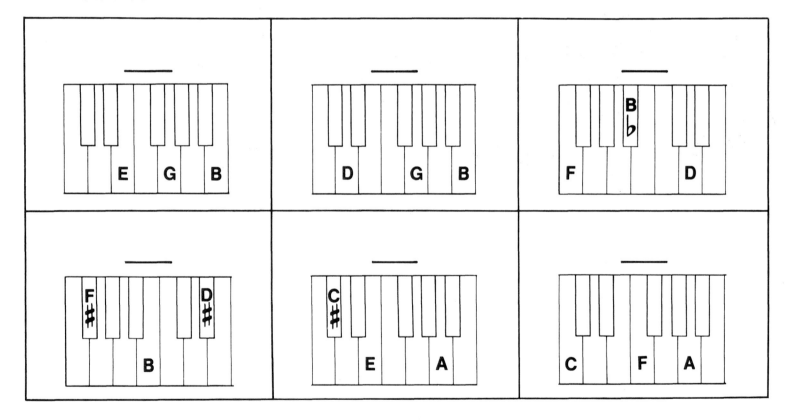

47. Write the name of the root above each triad. Circle each **second inversion triad.**

Use with pages 20-23, LESSONS, Level Four.

48. Write the first and second inversion for each given root position triad.

Matching Game

49. The triads below are in either the first or second inversion position. Write the number of each triad on the blank beside the matching definition.

1.

A. _____ A Major triad, FIRST INVERSION

2.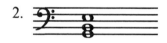

B. _____ D Minor triad, SECOND INVERSION

3.

C. _____ G Major triad, SECOND INVERSION

4.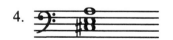

D. _____ C Minor triad, FIRST INVERSION

5.

E. _____ F Major triad, SECOND INVERSION

6.

F. _____ E Minor triad, FIRST INVERSION

Use with page 24, LESSONS, Level Four.

Grace Note

The GRACE NOTE is written as a small eighth note and usually has a line drawn through it.

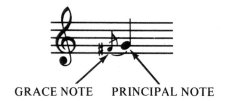

GRACE NOTE   PRINCIPAL NOTE

The grace note has no time value and is not counted as part of the rhythm.

50. Copy each grace note with its principal note in the blank measure beside it. Play these notes.

Rhythm Puzzle

51. Solve this puzzle by filling in the blanks of the clues. Choose the answers from the words in the box.

ANSWERS:

SYNCOPATED, GRACE, FOUR,
SIXTEENTH, TRIPLET, EIGHTH

CLUES:

ACROSS:

3. _____ sixteenth notes equal one quarter note.

4. When a long note is played on the weak part of the beat, the rhythm is

_____ .

5. This (♪) is called a

_____ note.

6. Two sixteenth notes are equal in

value to one _____ note.

DOWN:

1. This rhythm pattern (♩ ♩ ♩) is called a _____ .

2. This note (♪) is a _____ note.

Use with pages 25-27, LESSONS, Level Four.

The Dotted Eighth Note

The dotted eighth note (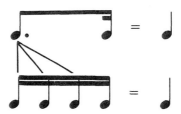) is equal in value to three sixteenth notes.
It is usually followed by a 16th note. The two notes are equal to one quarter note.

52. Clap and count aloud. (Your teacher will tell you how to count.)

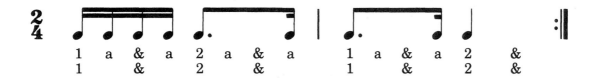

53. Write four groups of dotted eighth note patterns as shown in the example.

54. Write the counts under these notes.

55. Tap and count.

Use with pages 28-29, LESSONS, Level Four.

20 56. Add notes or rests to complete these measures.

57. Find the total number of beats of the notes in each box. Write that number on the line in the circle.

A.

B.

C.

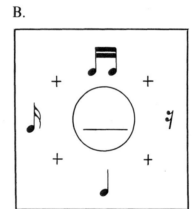

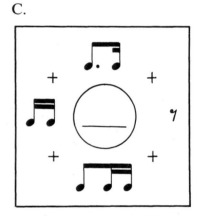

58. * Look and listen as your teacher plays one of the rhythm patterns in each line, A and B. Which pattern do you hear? Circle 1 or 2.

1.   2.

A.

1.   2.

B.

Use with pages 28-29, LESSONS, Level Four.

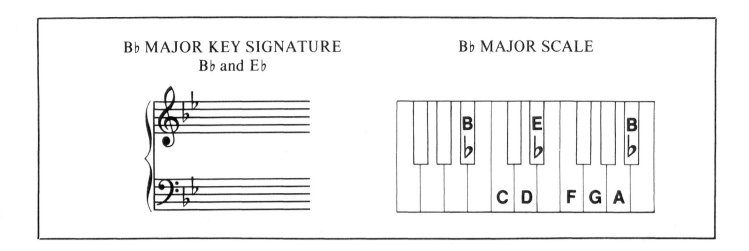

59. Write the B♭ Major key signature at the beginning of each staff.

60. Use quarter notes to write the ascending B♭ Major scale. Play each scale, ascending and descending.

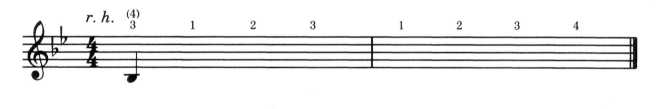

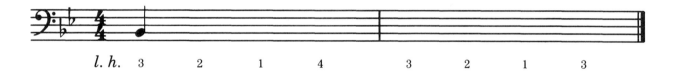

61. Play this scale piece.

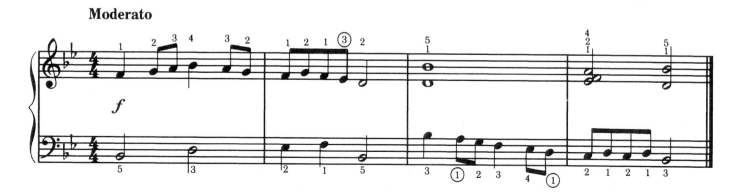

Use with page 30, LESSONS, Level Four.

Primary Chords in B♭ Major

62. Play these primary chords in the key of B♭ Major.

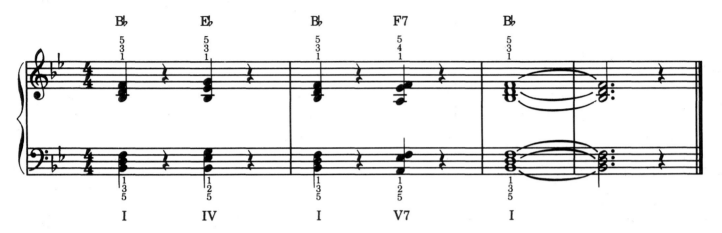

63. Copy the primary chords shown above as indicated by the Roman numerals and chord letter names. Use quarter notes.

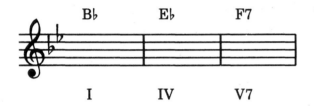

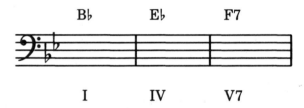

64. Write the notes of the **first inversion** and **second inversion chords** for the root position B♭ Major triad. Play the root position and both inversions with each hand.

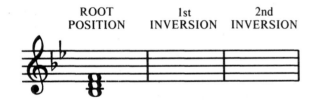

65. Harmonize this B♭ Major scale by playing the primary chords with the left hand as indicated.

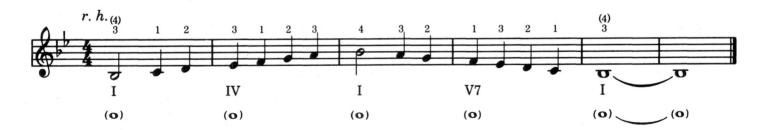

Use with page 30, LESSONS, Level Four.

66. Use the words found in the "water spray" to answer the clues and solve the puzzle.

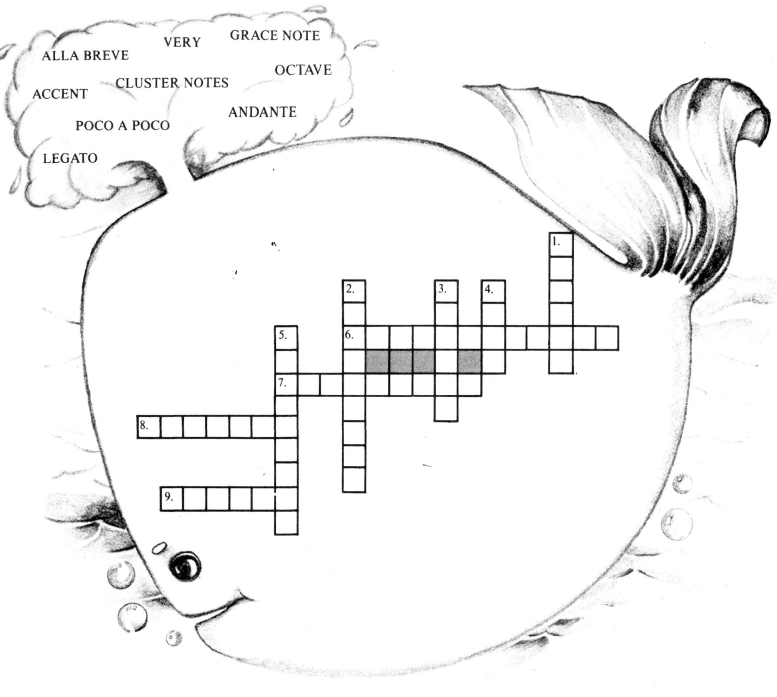

Words in the "water spray":
GRACE NOTE, VERY, ALLA BREVE, OCTAVE, ACCENT, CLUSTER NOTES, ANDANTE, POCO A POCO, LEGATO

CLUES:

DOWN:

1. _____ means to play smoothly.
2. _____ _____ _____ means "little by little."
3. This (*8va*) is an _____ sign.
4. Molto means _____,or much.
5. A_____ _____ is played quickly before the principal note. It has no time value.

ACROSS:

6. Undesignated notes played as a group are called _____ _____ .
7. This symbol (¢) indicates "cut time" or _____ _____ .
8. _____ means a walking speed.
9. *sfz* means to play with a strong _____ .

Use with pages 31-33, LESSONS, Level Four.

67. Find the minor scale related to B♭ Major. Circle the 6th tone of the B♭ Major Scale.

68. The name of that note is _____ .

69. The relative minor scale to B♭ Major is _____ minor.

70. Use quarter notes to write the ascending G **natural minor scale.** Play.

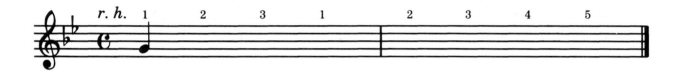

71. On the keyboard write the letter names of the G **natural minor scale.**

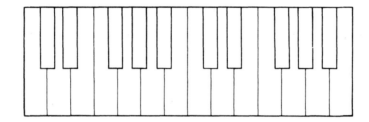

72. Use quarter notes to write the ascending G **harmonic minor scale.** Play this scale.

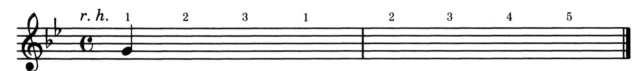

73. On the keyboard write the letter names of the G **harmonic minor scale.**

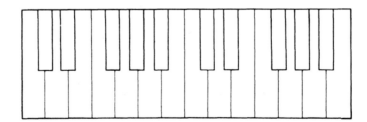

74. Use quarter notes to draw the G **melodic minor scale** ascending and descending. Play.

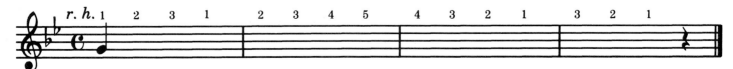

Use with pages 34-35, LESSONS, Level Four.

Primary Chords in G Minor

75. Play this G minor chord progression.

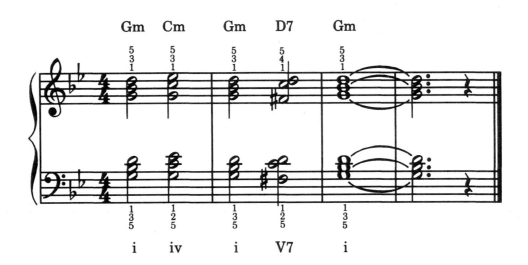

76. Fill in the blanks. All answers relate to Primary Chords in the key of G Minor.

A. This (🎼) is the _____ (i, iv, or V7) chord in the key of G minor.

B. The letter names of the notes of the V7 chord are _____ , _____ , and _____ .

C. The chord letter name of the i chord is _____ (Gm, Cm, or D7).

D. This (🎼) is the _____ (i, iv or V7) chord in the key of G Minor.

E. The letter names of the notes of the iv chord are _____ , _____ , and _____ .

F. This (🎼) is the _____ (i, iv, or V7) chord in the key of G minor.

G. The chord letter name of the V7 chord is _____ (Gm, Cm, or D7).

H. The letter names of the notes of the i chord are _____ , _____ , and _____ .

I. The chord letter name of the iv chord is _____ (Gm, Cm, or D7).

Use with pages 34-35, LESSONS, Level Four.

Rhythm Review

77. Clap these rhythm patterns while counting aloud.

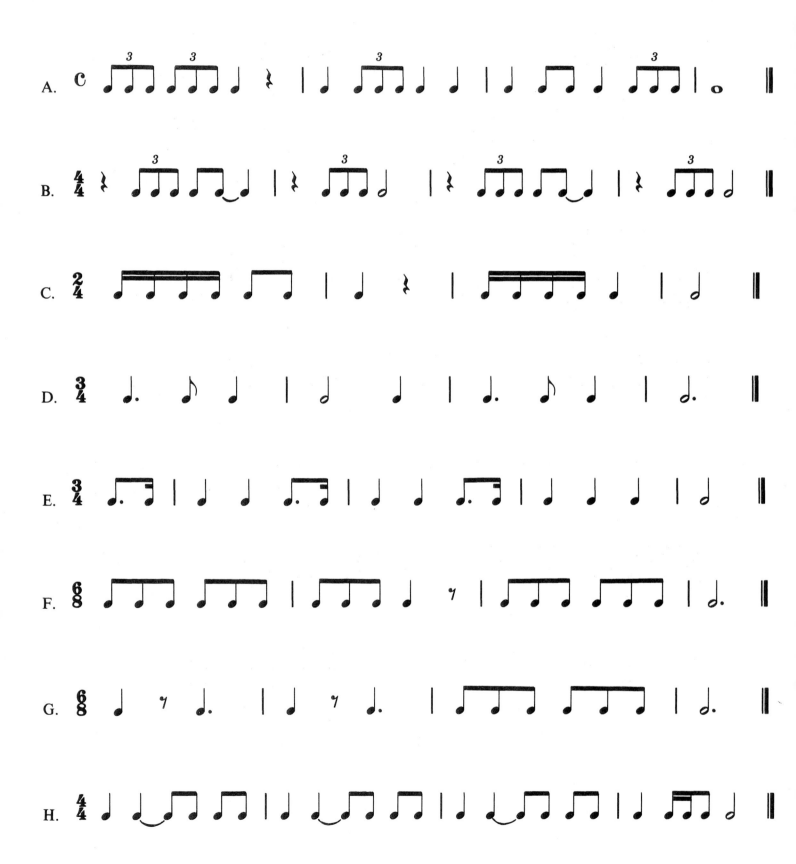

Key of Eb Major

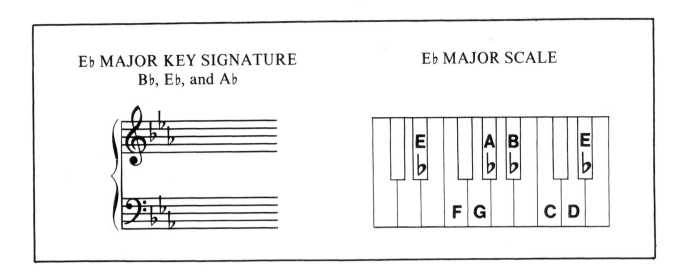

Eb MAJOR KEY SIGNATURE
Bb, Eb, and Ab

Eb MAJOR SCALE

78. Write the Eb Major key signature on each grand staff below.

79. Use quarter notes to write the ascending Eb Major scale. Play each scale ascending and descending.

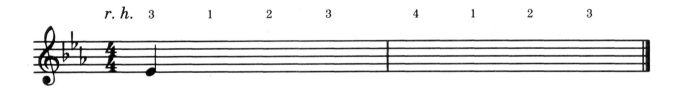

80. Fill in the blanks.

A. The key signature for Eb Major has _____ flats.

B. The notes that are flatted are named _____ , _____ , and _____ .

Use with pages 38-39, LESSONS, Level Four.

Primary Chords in E♭ Major

81.   Play these primary chords in the key of E♭ major.

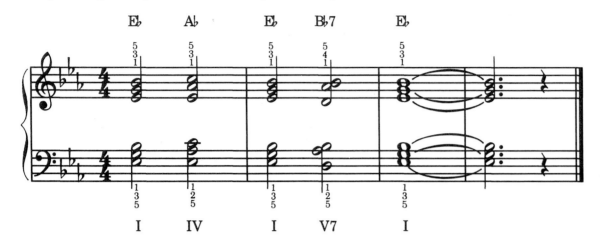

82.   Copy the primary chords shown above as indicated by the Roman numerals and chord letter names. Use whole notes.

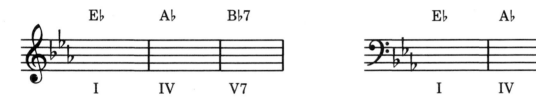

83.   Write the correct Roman numeral under each primary chord in E♭ Major.

84.   Write the notes on the staff and write the letter names on the keyboard to form the **root position, first inversion,** and **second inversion** of the E♭ Major triad.

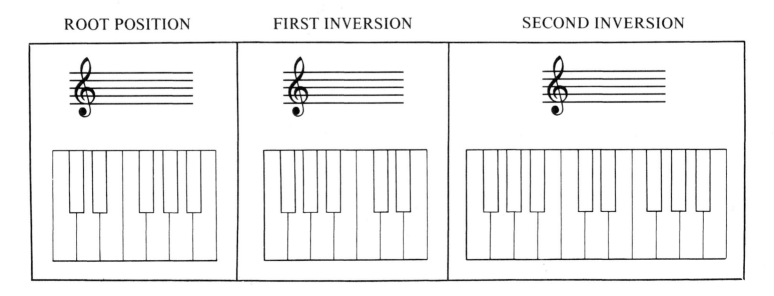

Use with pages 38-39, LESSONS, Level Four.

THREE NEW TERMS:

> ♪ ← This sign is a SLIGHT ACCENT mark. It means to accent the note slightly with a sustained quality.
>
> CANTABILE: play in a singing style.
>
> VIVACE: play with life, fast.

85. Complete this story by filling in the blanks. Choose your answers from the words on the dancer's shawl.

SPANISH DANCER

The lovely, dark-haired senorita walked _____ to the center of the room. Spanish men with
                                                  1. (Adagio)

guitars played flamenco music _____ _____ _____ _____ as she
                                    2. (cantabile)

began to dance. The dance began at _____ _____ _____ , then became
                                      3. (moderato)

_____ _____ until the music reached a _____ _____
4. (accelerando)   5. (allegro)

pace. Faster and faster the senorita whirled to the music, while clicking her heels and her castanets

loudly. Her dance was filled _____ _____ . Finally, she ended the dance with a flurry of
                                      6. (vivace)

twirls and taps. With her dark eyes flashing, the senorita bowed to the cheers of the audience and

demurely left the room.

WITH LIFE

FAST, BRISK

SLOWLY

IN A SINGING STYLE

A MODERATE SPEED

GRADUALLY FASTER

Use with pages 40-41, LESSONS, Level Four.

86. Find the minor scale related to E♭ Major. Circle the 6th tone of the E♭ Major scale.

87. The name of that note is _____ .

88. The relative minor scale to E♭ Major is _____ minor.

89. Use quarter notes to write the ascending C **natural minor scale.** Play this scale.

90. On the keyboard write the letter names of the C **natural minor scale.**

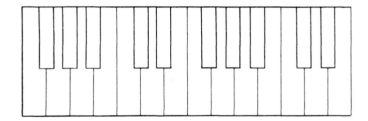

91. Use quarter notes to write the ascending C **harmonic minor scale.** Play this scale.

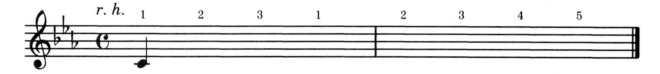

92. On the keyboard write the letter names of the C **harmonic minor scale.**

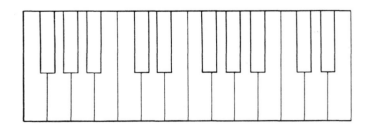

93. Use quarter notes to write the C **melodic minor scale** ascending and descending. Play this scale.

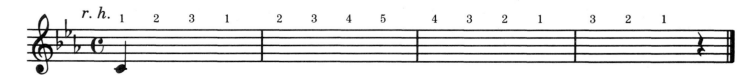

Use with pages 42-43, LESSONS, Level Four.

94. Play this C minor chord progression.

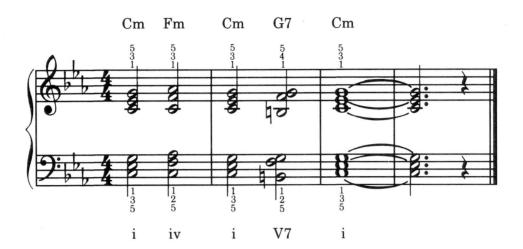

95. Write C minor (i) chords in the key of C minor, blocked or broken as indicated. Play.

BLOCKED   BROKEN   BLOCKED   BROKEN

96. Write F minor (iv) chords in the key of C minor, blocked or broken as indicated. Play.

BLOCKED   BROKEN   BLOCKED   BROKEN

97. Write G7 (V7) chords in the key of C minor, blocked or broken as indicated. Play.

BLOCKED   BROKEN   BLOCKED   BROKEN

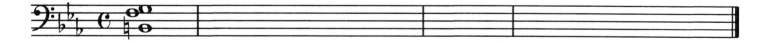

98. Tap and count.

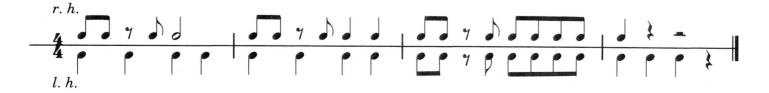

Use with pages 42-43, LESSONS, Level Four.

Minor Key Signatures

There is a major key name and a
minor key name for every key signature.

To decide whether a piece is **major** or **minor,** (1) look at the beginning and ending notes (the ending note is usually the key note or a note in the I [or i] chord of that key), and (2) play the piece to listen for a major or a minor sound.

99.   Play this piece and fill in the blanks below.

    A. The key signature of this piece could be either _____ major or _____ minor.

    B. The beginning and ending notes are _____ .

    C. The piece has a _____ sound. (major or minor)

    D. The key is _____ _____ .

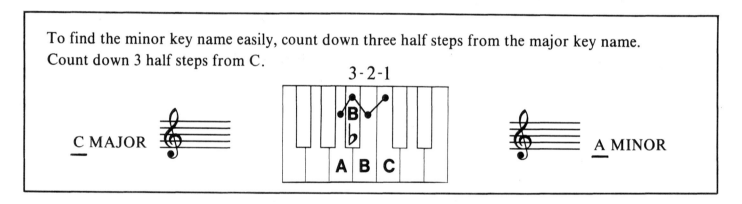

To find the minor key name easily, count down three half steps from the major key name. Count down 3 half steps from C.

100.   On the blank at the left, write the name of the major key signature. On the keyboard, count down 3 half steps to find the name of the minor key signature. On the blank at the right, write the name of the minor key signature. (See example above.)

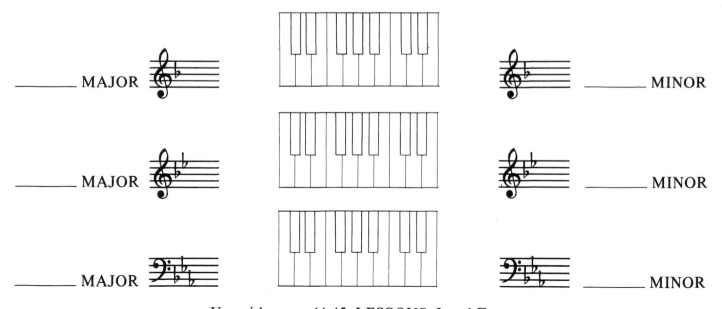

Use with pages 44-45, LESSONS, Level Four.

Augmented Triads

AUGMENT means to make larger.

A major triad becomes an AUGMENTED (larger) triad when the top note (the 5th) is raised one half step.

C MAJOR TRIAD   C AUGMENTED TRIAD (C aug. or C +)

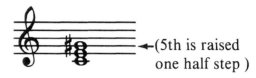

←(5th is raised one half step)

The AUGMENTED triad may be indicated by the abbreviation **aug** or the symbol + following the chord letter name.

101.   Change these major triads to AUGMENTED triads by raising the top note, or the 5th, one half step. Play these chords.

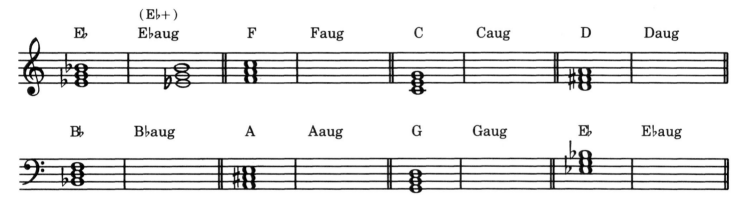

102.   On each keyboard below, write the letter names of the augmented triad as indicated.

F AUGMENTED TRIAD   C AUGMENTED TRIAD   G AUGMENTED TRIAD

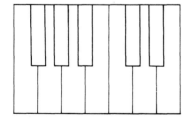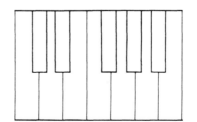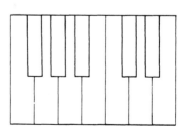

* 103.   Listen as your teacher plays a major triad or augmented triad. Circle the one you hear.

A. major   B. major   C. major

augmented   augmented   augmented

Use with pages 46-47, LESSONS, Level Four.

Diminished Triads

DIMINISH means to make smaller.

A minor triad becomes a DIMINISHED (smaller) triad when the top note (the 5th) is lowered one half step.

A MINOR TRIAD  A DIMINISHED TRIAD (A dim or A°)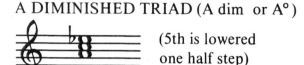

(5th is lowered one half step)

The DIMINISHED triad may be indicated by the abbreviation **dim** or the symbol ° following the chord letter name.

104. Change these minor triads to DIMINISHED triads by lowering the top note, or the 5th, one half step. Play these chords.

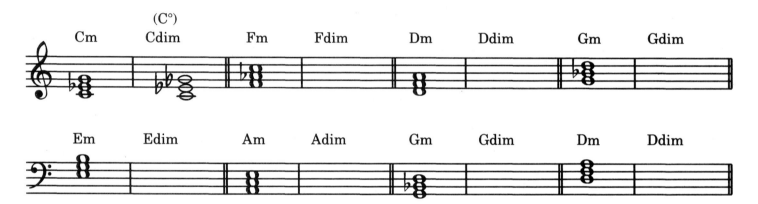

105. On each keyboard below, write the letter names of the diminished triad as indicated.

D DIMINISHED TRIAD   A DIMINISHED TRIAD   E DIMINISHED TRAID

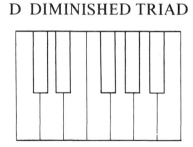 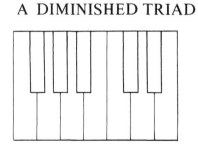 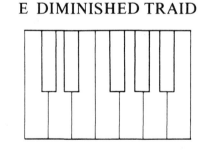

*106. Listen as your teacher plays a minor triad or diminished triad. Circle the one you hear.

A. minor   B. minor   C. minor

   diminished   diminished   diminished

Use with pages 48-49, LESSONS, Level Four.

More Augmented and Diminished Triads

107. Circle each AUGMENTED triad and write its chord letter name above it.

108. Circle each DIMINISHED triad and write its chord letter name above it.

109. Write two more notes to form a diminished triad above each given root note. Play these diminished triads.

110. Match each triad with its correct name.

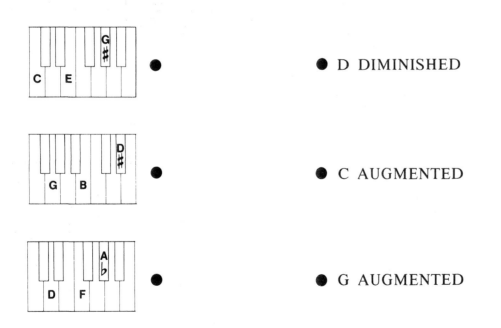

* 111. Listen as your teacher plays a group of three triads. Circle the group you hear.

A.   major - major - augmented   OR   minor - minor - diminished

B.   minor - diminished - minor   OR   major - augmented - major

Use after page 49, LESSONS, Level Four.

Major Sharp Key Signatures

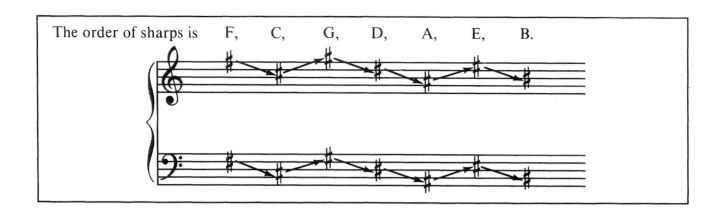

112. Write the sharps in their correct order on each grand staff.

To find the name of a major sharp key, name the last sharp to the right, then go up one half step. THIS IS THE NAME OF THE MAJOR SHARP KEY.

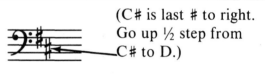

(C# is last # to right. Go up ½ step from C# to D.)

KEY OF D MAJOR

113. Circle the last sharp to the right in each key signature. Write the key-note one half step above the circled sharp. Write the name of each key signature on the blank.

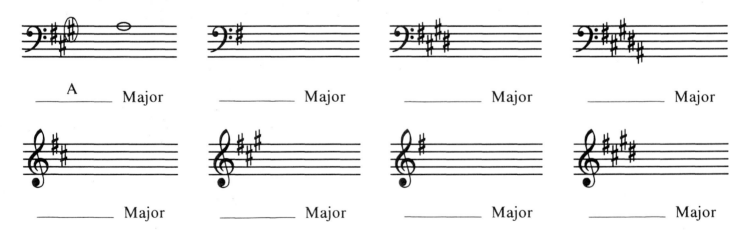

____A____ Major   _____ Major   _____ Major   _____ Major

_____ Major   _____ Major   _____ Major   _____ Major

114. Fill in the blanks.
    The order of sharps is _____ , _____ , _____ , _____ , _____ , _____ , _____ .

Use with page 50, LESSONS, Level Four.

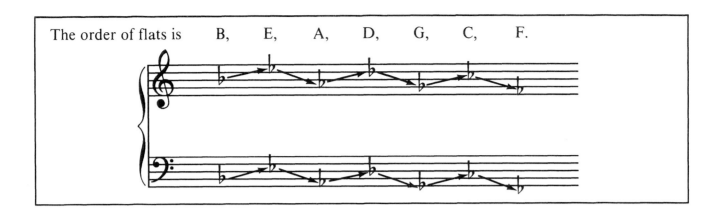

The order of flats is   B,   E,   A,   D,   G,   C,   F.

115.   Write the flats in their correct order on each grand staff.

To find the name of a major flat key, name the next to the last flat to the right. THIS IS THE NAME OF THE MAJOR FLAT KEY, EXCEPT for the key of F Major, which has only one flat, B♭.

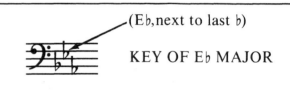

(E♭, next to last ♭)

KEY OF E♭ MAJOR

116.   Circle the next to the last flat to the right in each key signature. Write the key note on the staff, and write the name of each key signature on the blank.

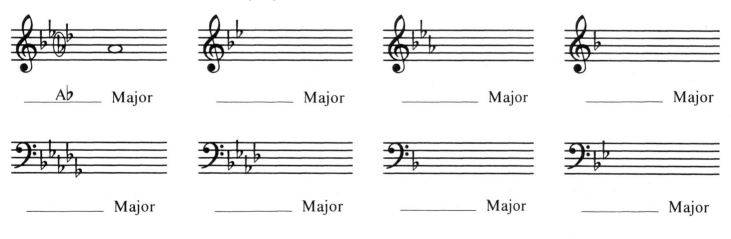

_____A♭_____ Major   _____ Major   _____ Major   _____ Major

_____ Major   _____ Major   _____ Major   _____ Major

117.   Fill in the blanks.
The order of flats is _____ , _____ , _____ , _____ , _____ , _____ , _____ .

NOTE: The order of flats is OPPOSITE to the order of sharps!

Use with page 50, LESSONS, Level Four.

Major Key Signatures (Review)

118. Name the clowns by identifying the Major Key signatures found in the "juggling balls." (See example.)

Example:

<u>E♭</u> <u>D</u>
1.   2.

A. ___ ___ N ___ I ___ ___
   1. 2.   3.   4.   5.

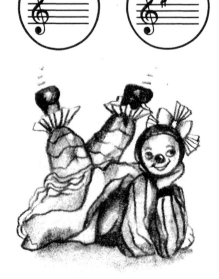

B. ___ R ___ ♭ ___
  1. 2.   3.

C. ___ R ___ I ___
  1. 2.   3.

D. ___ ♭ ___ R ___ I ___
  1. 2.   3.   4.

Use with page 50, LESSONS, Level Four.

Name the Scales

Name the Scales 39

119. Play each scale. On the line before the scale, write its name.

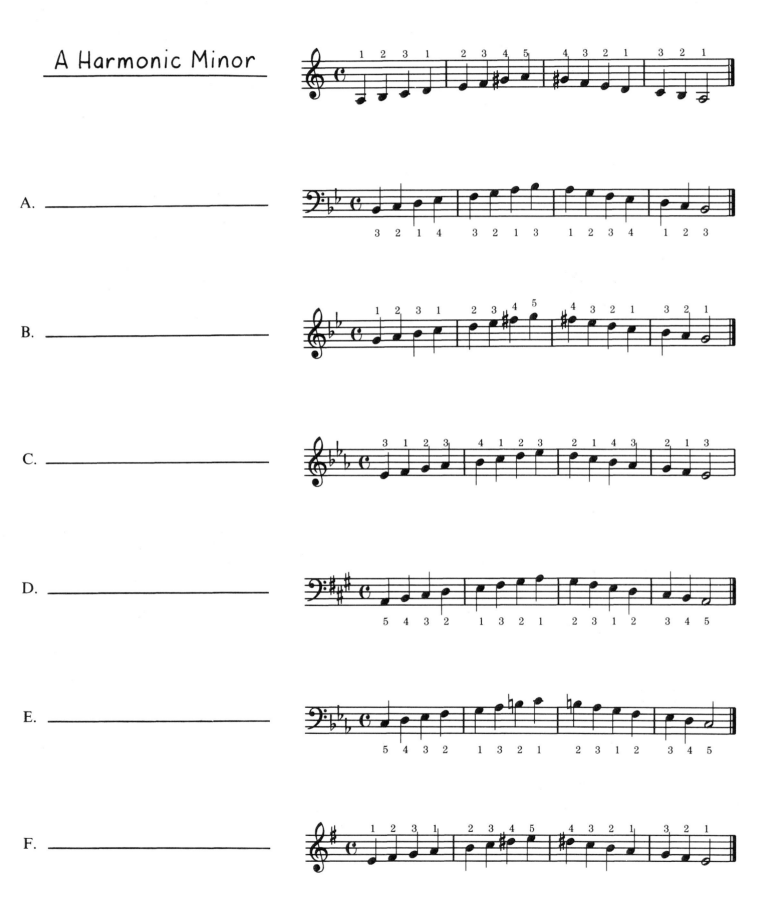

A Harmonic Minor

A. _____

B. _____

C. _____

D. _____

E. _____

F. _____

Use with pages 51-54, LESSONS, Level Four.

Name the Chord Progression

120. Play each chord progression below. Write its name on the blank beside it.

i   iv   i   V7   i

A Minor

A.

i   iv   i   V7   i

_____

B.

I   IV   I   V7   I

_____

C.

I   IV   I   V7   I

_____

D.

i   iv   i   V7   i

_____

E.

I   IV   I   V7   I

_____

F.

i   iv   i   V7   i

_____

Use with pages 51-56, LESSONS, Level Four.

121. Below the boxes write the pairs of numbers that match. (See example.)

A.

2.	1. 2nd Inversion Triad
	3.
4. 1st Inversion Triad	

A. ___*1*___ and ___*2*___ , ___*3*___ and ___*4*___

B.

1.	¢
2.	Common Time
3.	**C**
4.	Alla Breve

B. _____ and _____ , _____ and _____

C.

1.	(music notation)
2.	E♭ MAJOR SCALE
3.	C HARMONIC MINOR SCALE
4.	(music notation)

C. _____ and _____ , _____ and _____

D.

2.	1. Augmented Triad
	3.
	4. Diminished Triad

D. _____ and _____ , _____ and _____

E.

2.	1. Key of D MAJOR
	3.
4. Key of A MAJOR	

E. _____ and _____ , _____ and _____

F.

1.	With spirit
2.	*Con brio*
3.	*Cantabile*
4.	In a singing style

F. _____ and _____ , _____ and _____

Use with page 57, LESSONS, Level Four.

* Listen as your teacher plays. Circle the correct answer.

122. Which rhythm pattern do you hear? Circle A or B.

123. This minor scale is   A. natural   B. harmonic   C. melodic

124. This minor scale is   A. natural   B. harmonic   C. melodic

125. This minor scale is   A. natural   B. harmonic   C. melodic

126. This triad is   A. augmented   B. diminished

127. This triad is   A. augmented   B. diminished

128. Which melody do you hear? Circle A or B.

129. Which rhythm pattern do you hear? Circle A or B.

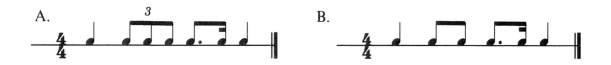

Use with page 57, LESSONS, Level Four.

1.
A.	Slow tempo	4	K.	Moderate tempo	19
B.	Very loud	17	L.	Moderately soft	15
C.	ABA form	10	M.	Gradually slower	2
D.	Staccato note	9	N.	Moderately loud	12
E.	Common time	14	O.	Fast, brisk tempo	5
F.	Very soft	18	P.	Gradually louder	6
G.	Fermata	13	Q.	Accented note	8
H.	Added ending	16	R.	Return to original speed	1
I.	Gradually softer	3	S.	Triplet	7
J.	With expression	11			

PAGE 4

2. A HARMONIC MINOR SCALE. Student plays.

3.

i   iv   i   V7   i

4. Student taps and counts as directed.

5.

1st   2nd   2nd   Root   1st   Root   1st

PAGE 5

6.
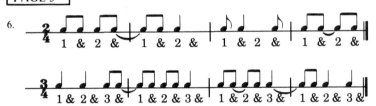

7. Student plays and harmonizes melody as directed.

PAGE 6

8.

9.

PAGE 7

10.

1 a & a 2 &   1 a & a 2 &

or as directed by teacher.

11. Student taps and counts as directed.

12.
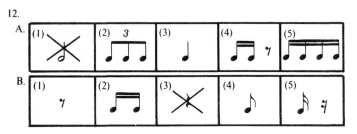

PAGE 7 (cont.)

* TEACHER'S LISTENING EXAMPLES:

13.
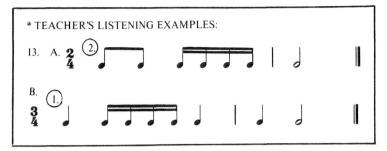

PAGE 8

14.
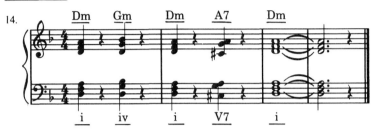

i   iv   i   V7   i

15.

16. A. The key signature for the key of D minor is one flat. (or B Flat.)

    B. The relative Major key for D minor is F Major.

17. Student plays chords as indicated.

PAGE 9

18.

19.

20. The key signature for A Major has 3 sharps. The notes that are sharped are named F, C and G.

PAGE 10

21. Student plays chords as directed.

44

PAGE 10 (cont.)

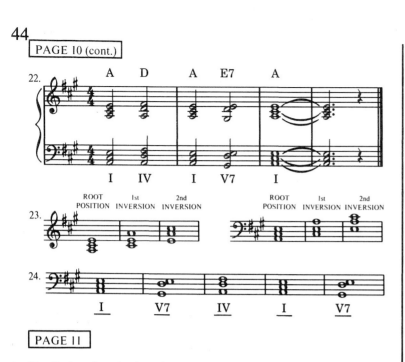

22.

23. | ROOT POSITION | 1st INVERSION | 2nd INVERSION | | ROOT POSITION | 1st INVERSION | 2nd INVERSION |

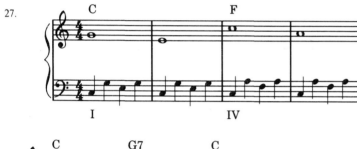

24.

PAGE 11

25. Student plays chords as directed.

26. Student plays and transposes as directed.

27.

PAGE 12

28.
29.
30.

PAGE 13

31.

32. E

33.

34.

35.

36.

PAGE 14

37.

38.   39.

*TEACHER'S LISTENING EXAMPLE

40.   TEACHER PLAYS IN THIS ORDER

1. C.   E NATURAL MINOR SCALE

2. A.   E HARMONIC MINOR SCALE

3. B.   E MELODIC MINOR SCALE

PAGE 15

41.
i   iv   V

42. Student plays as directed.

43.

iv   i   iv   V7   i   V7   iv   i

44.
Em   Am   B7   Em

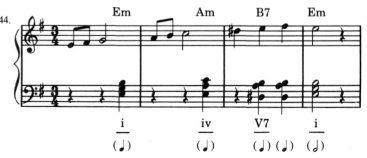

i   iv   V7   i
(♩)   (♩)   (♩)(♩)(♩)

45

PAGE 16

45.
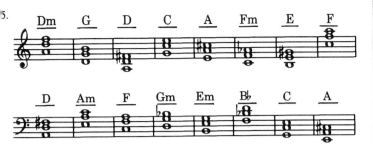

46.
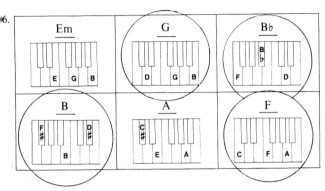

47.
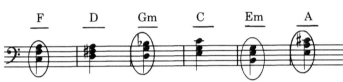

PAGE 17

48.
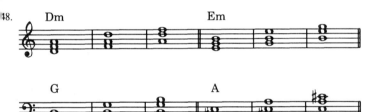

49. A. 4, B. 5, C. 1, D. 6, E. 3, F. 2.

PAGE 18

50.

51. DOWN: 1. triplet, 2. sixteenth.

ACROSS: 3. Four, 4. syncopated, 5. grace, 6. eighth.

PAGE 19

52. Student claps and counts as teacher directs.

53.

54.
1 a & a 2 a & a   1 a & a 2 &

55. Student taps and counts.

PAGE 20

56. Other combinations possible.

57. A. 3, B. 2, C. 3

* 58. TEACHER'S LISTENING EXAMPLE

PAGE 21

59.

60.
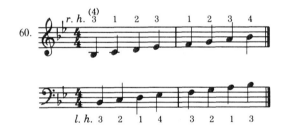

61. Student plays piece as directed.

PAGE 22

62. Student plays chords as directed.

63.
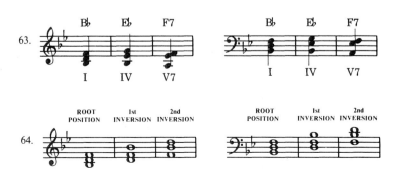

64.

65. Student harmonizes scale as directed.

PAGE 23

66. DOWN: 1. legato, 2. poco a poco, 3. octave,
4. very, 5. grace note

ACROSS: 6. cluster notes, 7. alla breve, 8. andante, 9. accent

PAGE 24

67.

68. The name of this note is <u>G</u>.

69. <u>G</u> Minor

70.

71.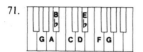

72.

73.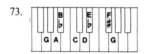

74.

PAGE 25

75. Student plays chord progression.

76. A. iv
B. F#, C, and D
C. Gm
D. V7
E. G, C, and E♭
F. i
G. D7
H. G, B♭, and D
I. Cm

PAGE 26

77. Student claps rhythm patterns.

PAGE 27

78.

79.

80. A. three. B. B, E, and A.

PAGE 28

81. Student plays chords as directed.

82.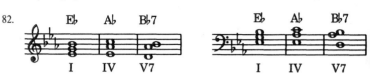

83.

84.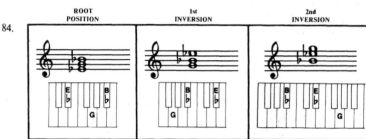

PAGE 29

85. 1. slowly, 2. in a singing style,
3. a moderate speed, 4. gradually faster,
5. fast, brisk, 6. with life.

PAGE 30

86.

87. The name of this note is <u>C</u>.

88. The relative minor scale to E♭ Major is <u>C</u> Minor.

89.

90.

91.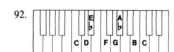

92.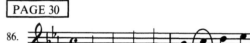

93.

PAGE 31

94. Student plays chord progression.

47

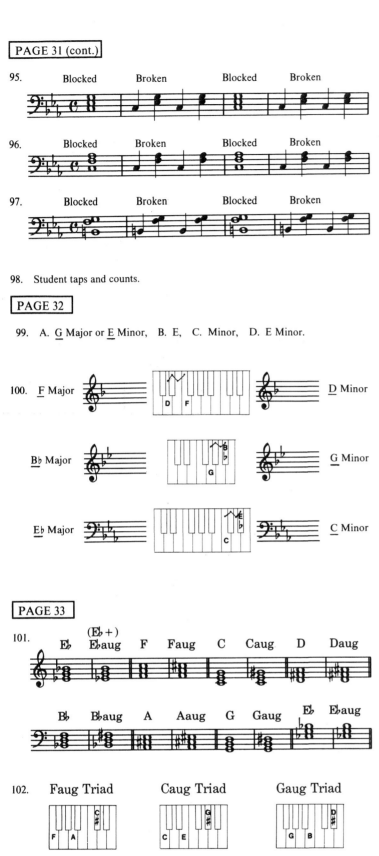
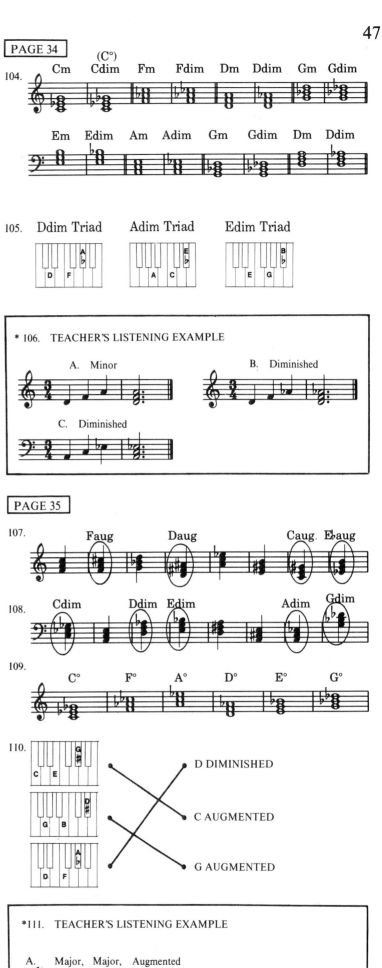
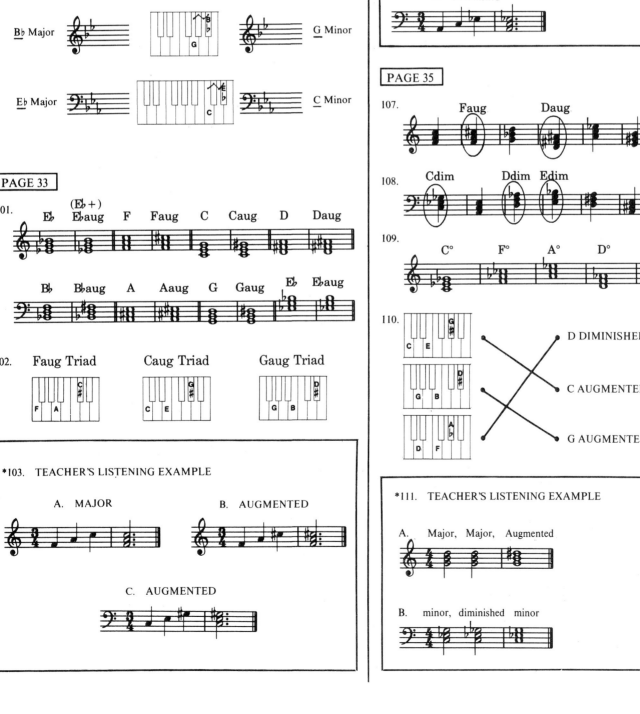

48

PAGE 36

112.

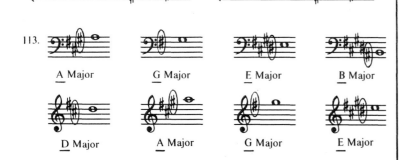

113.

A Major   G Major   E Major   B Major

D Major   A Major   G Major   E Major

114. F, C, G, D, A, E, and B.

PAGE 37

115.

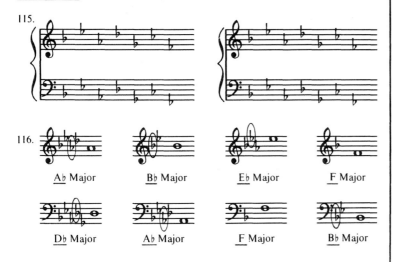

116.

Ab Major   Bb Major   Eb Major   F Major

Db Major   Ab Major   F Major   Bb Major

117. B, E, A, D, G, C, F.

PAGE 38

118. A. CANDICE, B. FRED, C. CRAIG, D. BARBIE

PAGE 39

119. A. Bb MAJOR, B. G HARMONIC MINOR,
     C. Eb MAJOR, D. A MAJOR, E. C HARMONIC MINOR
     F. E HARMONIC MINOR

PAGE 40

120.

A minor
   i   iv   i   V7   i

A.

G minor
      i   iv   i   V7   i

B.

Bb Major
   I   IV   I   V7   I

C.

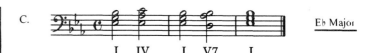

Eb Major
   I   IV   I   V7   I

D.

C minor
      i   iv   i   V7   i

E.

A Major
   I   IV   I   V7   I

F.

E minor
      i   iv   i   V7   i

PAGE 41

121. B. 1 and 4, 2 and 3,   C. 1 and 3, 2 and 4,
      D. 1 and 2, 3 and 4,   E. 1 and 3, 2 and 4,
      F. 1 and 2, 3 and 4

PAGE 42

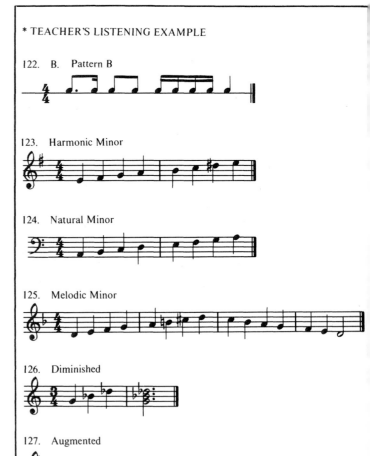

* TEACHER'S LISTENING EXAMPLE

122. B. Pattern B

123. Harmonic Minor

124. Natural Minor

125. Melodic Minor

126. Diminished

127. Augmented

128. Melody B

129. A. Pattern A